# Role Models

# WONDROUS
# WOMEN
— WHO —
# CHANGED
— THE —
# WORLD

**Thunder Bay Press**
An imprint of Printers Row Publishing Group
10350 Barnes Canyon Road, Suite 100, San Diego, CA 92121
www.thunderbaybooks.com • mail@thunderbaybooks.com

Printers Row Publishing Group is a division of Readerlink Distribution Services, LLC.
Thunder Bay Press is a registered trademark of Readerlink Distribution Services, LLC.

Correspondence regarding the content of this book should be
addressed to Thunder Bay Press, Editorial Department, at the above address.
Correspondence regarding author/illustration/rights/etc. should be addressed
to Quarto Publishing, The Old Brewery, 6 Blundell Street, London, N7 9BH, UK.

**Thunder Bay Press**
**Publisher:** Peter Norton • **Associate Publisher:** Ana Parker
**Senior Product Manager:** Kathryn C. Dalby
**Editor:** JoAnn Padgett

**Quarto Children's Books**
**Author:** Jenny Jacoby
**Illustrator:** Maëva Collet
**Paper Engineer:** A Bag of Badgers and Jayne Evans
**Editor:** Ellie Brough
**Designers:** Alan Brown and Mike Henson
**Publisher:** Jonathan Gilbert
**Contracts & Licensing Director:** Mozidur Rahman

ISBN: 978-1-68412-951-5
Printed in Shaoguan, China SL092019
23 22 21 20 19 1 2 3 4 5

# Role Models

# WONDROUS WOMEN WHO CHANGED THE WORLD

Written by
## JENNY JACOBY
Illustrated by
## MAËVA COLLET

# CONTENTS

# INTRODUCTION

There is something powerful about a woman who possesses the confidence of a man. She is an unexpected and incredibly underestimated force with the capability of changing perceptions, society, and the world.

But why is that so? Why was Amelia Earhart looked down upon by her grandmother for wanting to wear pants and climb trees like the boys of her age? Why was Rosalind Franklin's contribution to the discovery of the DNA model overlooked and ignored by the science community of her time? Why did Ruth Bader Ginsburg get demoted from her job, simply because she was pregnant with her first child? The simple answer is: because they are women.

For too long, women were, and still are, considered lesser in many respects to men. In some places in the world, they are second-class by law—their rights restricted when compared to their male peers. In other parts, though the law says men and women are equal, women still face limitations, prejudice, and discrimination. And yet, do they allow it? No. For as long as women have faced injustices, they have been standing up and fighting for recognition, equality, and fairness.

We don't remember Amelia Earhart as a little girl who was told not to wear pants. We remember her as one of the bravest and most fearless adventurers of all time. We don't allow Rosalind Franklin's achievements to go unwritten, but recall them and record them so her name and genius are not forgotten. We don't pity Ruth Bader Ginsburg for the way she was treated—we bow in the presence of her greatness and thank her for everything she has done to reverse laws of inequality in the United States.

These women are the role models that we need and deserve to allow us to grow up in, and help shape, a better world for girls everywhere. These are just some of their stories—read them, treasure them, and then build the ten models included to take with you as you create your own stories of inspiration.

# Georgia O'Keeffe

Georgia O'Keeffe is one of the most important artists of the twentieth century. She has been dubbed the "mother of American modernism."

Georgia grew up on a dairy farm in Wisconsin, and decided when she was ten that she wanted to be an artist. In 1905 she attended the Art Institute of Chicago, but when her father went bankrupt and her mother became seriously ill, she couldn't afford to stay.

She took up teaching. At an art class in 1912 she came across the work of Arthur Wesley Dow, which changed her approach to art. Before, she had been drawing from nature, copying its forms realistically. Now she realized that her art could be a form of self-expression and personal style.

Inspired, she completed a series of abstract drawings in charcoal, and Alfred Stieglitz exhibited them in his gallery in New York City. Stieglitz became a supportive friend who helped her career, and later they married.

Georgia was inspired by intense colors and the landscapes around her, whether the prairies or New York skyscrapers. She experimented with shapes and colors on a canvas until she felt she had captured her personal feelings in the image.

Georgia is most famous for her flowers—she made around 200 large-scale, closely cropped images of the insides of flowers. Her "Jimson Weed" painting of 1932 was commissioned for $10,000 and in 2014 it sold for $44,405,000—more than three times the record of any female artist.

Georgia painted throughout her long life. In 1946 she was the first female artist to have a retrospective at the Museum of Modern Art (MoMA) in New York City. In 1972 her eyesight started failing and she was no longer able to paint in oil, but she continued drawing until the end of her life. In 1977 she was awarded the Presidential Medal of Freedom, the highest honor for American civilians.

**1887** Born in Sun Prairie, Wisconsin, USA.

**1905** Enrolled at the Art Institute of Chicago.

**1911** Began teaching art.

**1915** Started producing abstract drawings.

**1916** First exhibited her art.

**1946** Had a retrospective at MoMA in New York City.

**1986** Died in New Mexico, USA.

# Yayoi Kusama

**Y**ayoi Kusama is Japan's most prominent contemporary artist. She overcame many difficulties to rise to fame in the 1960s and is best known for her repeating patterns, and her colorful clothes and bobbed wigs.

Born in 1929 to an affluent family, her childhood was not easy. She always knew she wanted to be a painter, and clearly had talent, but her mother took her inks and canvases away, telling her she had to marry someone rich and become a housewife.

When Yayoi was ten years old she started hallucinating flashes of light and fields of dots. She started painting as a way of coping with these intrusions in her mind—and this became the influence behind much of her work.

Although she did go to art school, she found the traditional Japanese art training too constricting, so she escaped to New York City. Arriving there she promised herself that she would conquer the city and make her name in the world. The New York City art scene was very male-dominated at that time, but she quickly became a key part of it, creating events called "happenings" in public spaces like Central Park, usually in protest of the Vietnam War.

She would spend all day painting repeating patterns and dots. She called her work "infinity nets," as the patterns would grow larger than the boundaries of the canvas and spill out onto the floors and walls. She also created infinity rooms using mirrored walls so the patterns looked as if they would go on forever.

But she painted herself to exhaustion and returned to Japan, ill, in 1973, starting her career anew in a country where her work was unknown.

Since 1977 she has chosen to live in a psychiatric institution, but every day she works in her studio. Her art helps the viewer experience her obsessive mind filled with endless dots. She has developed an artistic identity based partly on being an outsider: as a woman in a man's world, as a Japanese artist in the Western art world, and as someone living with mental ill health.

**1929**
Born in Nagano, Japan.

**1948**
Studied at Kyoto Municipal School of Arts and Crafts.

**1958**
Moved to New York City.

**1973**
Returned to Japan in ill health.

**2015**
50-year retrospective of her work held at Hirshhorn Museum, Washington, D.C.

**2017**
Yayoi Kusama museum opened in Tokyo.

# Frida Kahlo

Frida Kahlo was a Mexican painter born in Coyoacán, Mexico City, Mexico in 1907. She is well known for her colorful self-portraits often featuring herself in fantastical settings, surrounded by monkeys, and steeped in symbolism.

Two difficult things happened to Frida Kahlo when she was young that shaped her life as a woman and inspired her art. First, when she was six years old, she contracted polio, a disease that made her right leg shorter and thinner than the left. She had to wear a leg brace, which made her stand out from her school friends, and as a result, she was bullied and lonely.

Her disability never dampened her ambition though. Frida's father encouraged her in everything she did, supporting her pursuit of activities and interests that women at the time were not typically encouraged to do. Frida wanted to become a doctor, and it was when she was studying at a prestigious school, as one of only a few female students, that the second tragedy happened. She was traveling home when a car crashed into the bus she was on. She was impaled by a steel handrail that caused lasting damage to her spine and hips, which meant she could never have children. She survived, but she lived in pain for the rest of her life.

She gave up school while she recovered, spending months lying on her back, passing the time by painting. She had a special easel and a mirror on the ceiling so she could paint herself in bed. As her world shrank down to just her bedroom, Frida chose to paint what she could see, in the way she saw it: herself.

Over time Frida's art got better and better, and because she had always been encouraged to think for herself, she came up with her own way of telling her story. She did this in both her paintings and in her sense of style, portraying herself on canvas and in real life as a woman undefined by her physical limitations. No one else's paintings looked like hers and she became celebrated for her unique style. Nowadays, she is revered not only as a brilliant painter, but also as a fashion icon and a fierce feminist who created her own identity and refused to be ignored.

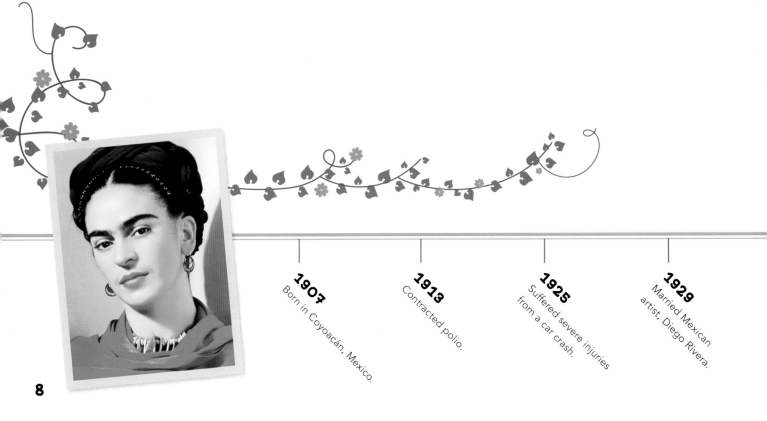

**1907**
Born in Coyoacán, Mexico.

**1913**
Contracted polio.

**1925**
Suffered severe injuries from a car crash.

**1929**
Married Mexican artist, Diego Rivera.

"I am my own muse.
I am the subject I
know best."

# Judy Chicago

**J**udy Chicago is an American artist who developed the ground-breaking Feminist Art Program at the California Institute of the Arts. Her work is famous for examining the role of women in history and culture.

Judy's parents were progressive for their times. Her father, Arthur, supported workers' and women's rights, and her mother gave her children a passion for the arts. Arthur was also a member of the American Communist Party, and was under investigation by the FBI, simply because of his political views. It was hard for him to find work, causing difficulty for the whole family.

Judy got a scholarship to study art at UCLA, where she met and married Jerry Gerowitz. When he died in a car crash two years later, Judy poured her grief into her work.

As Judy's career grew, she wanted a new name for herself—one that wasn't imposed on her by society's rules of male dominance. She rejected her family name, Cohen, and her late husband's name, Gerowitz. She chose Chicago because it was her home city, and was ethnically neutral.

In 1970 she started teaching a women's art class that developed into a full Feminist Art Program. Fueled by a desire to bring visibility to women in the art world, the courses were for women only and took place off-campus, where women could feel free to express themselves. The program encouraged women to develop their art, using their experiences as women.

In 1979 Judy completed her most famous work: a collaborative piece of installation art, and the first epic piece of feminist art: *The Dinner Party*. It addresses Judy's complaint that women have been written out of history. The installation is a triangular dinner party table set for thirty-nine historical female guests, including Georgia O'Keeffe, Sacagawea, and Mary Wollstonecraft.

Judy still creates images to redress the gender imbalance in art history.

**1939**
Born in Chicago, Illinois, USA.

**1964**
Received her Master of Fine Arts degree from UCLA, CA.

**1970**
Started teaching full-time at Fresno State College, CA.

**1979**
The Dinner Party was completed.

**1985**
Birth Project was completed.

**2012**
Awarded Lifetime Achievement Award at Palm Springs Art Fair.

# Pocahontas

Pocahontas was the daughter of the chief of the Powhatan tribes. "Pocahontas" was a nickname meaning "playful one." It was her playful nature and passionate kindness that earned her a place in both American and English history.

When Pocahontas was a little girl in the early seventeenth century, a group of English people sailed to her home, a place we know now as Virginia. The incomers built a fort and named their settlement "Jamestown," after the King of England. The English and the Native Americans had to get to know each other and try to share the land—this did not always go well.

One day, when the English were out hunting, the Powhatan captured a man named John Smith. Then, as he described in a letter to Queen Anne years later, just as several men were about to kill him with clubs, Pocahontas cradled his head in her arms and put her own head on top, saving his life. Then she persuaded her father to let Smith return to Jamestown.

Pocahontas made friends at Jamestown. Being strangers in a new environment, the English didn't always know how to find food. Pocahontas would bring them food every week or so, saving more lives.

When they were strong again, the English tried to take more land, which led to a war with the Powhatan. The English captured Pocahontas and held her for a year. She learned about Christianity and when she was allowed to see her people, she said she wanted to stay with the English "who loved her." She was cross with her father for letting her be a tool for negotiating in the war.

Living with the English, she was baptized and took the name "Rebecca." She married another Englishman, John Rolfe, and their marriage led to eight years of peace and trading between the English and Powhatan. Pocahontas and Rolfe had a son in 1615. They sailed for England to visit London and were guests at royal events. But before they could return to Virginia, Pocahontas died, aged about 21, and was buried at Gravesend, Kent.

**1595**
The likely year of Pocahontas's birth.

**1607**
Met and rescued John Smith.

**1609**
War broke out between the English settlers and the Powhatans.

**1613**
Captured by the English.

**1614**
Married the Englishman, John Rolfe.

**1616**
Traveled to England with her husband and child.

**1617**
Died in Gravesend, UK.

# Queen Elizabeth I

Queen Elizabeth I ruled England and Ireland for forty-four years. She reigned over a long period of prosperity—known as the Golden Age of England.

Elizabeth was the daughter of King Henry VIII of England and his second wife, Anne Boleyn. When Elizabeth was two years old, her father had Anne tried for treason and beheaded. He did this to end their marriage because she had not given birth to a son to be the future king—only one daughter, Elizabeth.

When Henry VIII died, Elizabeth's half-brother Edward and then her older half-sister Mary reigned. Queen Mary was Catholic, and she mistrusted Elizabeth because she was Protestant, so Elizabeth was imprisoned for almost a year.

When Queen Mary died, Elizabeth became queen. Once again England became a Protestant country.

Because her father left the Roman Catholic Church, the Pope declared Elizabeth illegitimate. This meant that many people in England did not believe she was the rightful queen and there were many plots to kill her. She had a trusted secret service that defeated each plot.

Elizabeth chose to rule by the motto "video et taceo," which means "I see but say nothing."

She delicately handled relationships with France and Spain. Both countries wooed Elizabeth, wanting to bring England into alliance with them and overpower the other country. Elizabeth did not want to favor either country and avoided marriage. She managed to maintain England as a powerful nation in its own right.

Between 1585 and 1604 Spain and England were informally at war—Philip of Spain had sworn to put a Catholic monarch on the throne in England. In 1588 Spain sent an armada of ships to attack England, but the English managed to disperse the ships.

Elizabeth was celebrated during her reign, which became known as the Elizabethan era. England's national identity strengthened under Elizabeth. Going to the theater became popular and playwrights such as Christopher Marlowe and William Shakespeare became famous. Under Elizabeth, English ships sailed around the world and increased trade routes.

When she died, some people were pleased to have a new king, but King James seemed disappointing after Elizabeth, and many looked back on the Elizabethan era with nostalgia.

**1533**
Born in London, UK.

**1536**
Her mother, Anne Boleyn, was beheaded.

**1547**
Her father, Henry VIII, died.

**1554**
Imprisoned in the Tower of London.

"I don't want a husband who honors me as a queen if he doesn't love me as a woman."

**1558**
Crowned Queen.

**1570**
Excommunicated by the Catholic Church.

**1588**
Spanish Armada attacked England.

**1601**
Died in Richmond, UK.

13

# Benazir Bhutto

enazir Bhutto was a politician and the first woman prime minister of any Muslim country. She was a secular leader in a strongly religious country and tried to modernize and advance women's rights. After falling out of favor with the government, she was assassinated in 2007.

Benazir was born in Karachi, the largest city in Pakistan. Her family was wealthy and involved in politics. Her father was in the government and, growing up, Benazir was used to politicians visiting their home. She was very close to her father and he encouraged her education, which was rare for women in Pakistan at the time.

When she was thirteen, her father set up the Pakistan People's Party (PPP), which aimed to be democratic, socialist, and Islamic. Benazir immediately joined.

Benazir studied at Harvard and the University of Oxford. She was the first Asian woman to be president of the Oxford Union debating society.

In 1971 her father became President of Pakistan, and then Prime Minister, but was ousted in a military coup in 1977. He was executed in 1979. Benazir and her mother were imprisoned for a year. They later took control of the PPP, but Benazir was repeatedly imprisoned, and then eventually exiled to the UK.

There, she was influenced by Margaret Thatcher, and returned to Pakistan in 1986 with progressive ideas. She reformed the PPP away from socialist principles to liberal ones, and in 1988 her party won the election. She was the first female prime minister in Pakistan, as well as the fourth and youngest in the world.

Huge opposition to a female prime minister meant Benazir couldn't advance her progressive causes very far. She created a women's division in government, set up a women's bank, and set up all-female police stations.

She also cofounded the Council of Women World Leaders, making a positive difference on the world stage.

**1953**
Born in Karachi, Pakistan.

**1979**
Her father was executed.

**1984**
Exiled to the UK.

**1986**
Returned to Pakistan.

**1988**
Became the first female prime minister of Pakistan.

**2007**
Assassinated in Rawalpindi, Pakistan.

# Margaret Thatcher

Margaret Thatcher was the first female prime minister of the United Kingdom, and the longest serving British prime minister of the twentieth century. She grew up in the apartment adjoining her father's grocery shop in a small town in northern England. As a girl she worked hard and won a scholarship to a grammar school (a high school with an entrance exam). She got her first taste of leadership when she became head girl there in her final year.

Margaret studied chemistry at the University of Oxford, but even then was becoming more interested in law and politics instead of science as a career. Later, while she was proud of becoming the first female prime minister, she said she was more proud of becoming the first prime minister with a science degree.

a powerful leader of an otherwise entirely male cabinet. A Soviet journalist nicknamed her the "Iron Lady," and the phrase became synonymous with her for her uncompromising politics and strong will.

Her time as leader radically changed Britain through the 1980s and into the future. She was in power during the last decade of the Cold War, a time of huge global tension, and she was a visible presence around the world. She was commonly thought of as the most powerful woman in the world—which, for the daughter of a grocer in a world dominated by expensively educated men, was an impressive journey.

> "In politics, if you want anything said, ask a man; if you want anything done, ask a woman."

As a young politician, Margaret became well known for her fearless way of speaking to the public and her fellow politicians. However, it took some time for her to be voted in as a member of Parliament, and in the meantime, she passed her qualification to be a barrister, as well as giving birth to twin children—showing how her hard work and determination brought results.

She became leader of the Conservative Party in 1975, and in 1979 her party won the general election. She brought in sweeping changes to British society and her politics polarized the country, but she held strong to her own beliefs. Despite much opposition, she remained

**1925**
Born in Lincolnshire, UK.

**1959**
Elected Conservative MP for Finchley.

**1975**
Elected leader of the Conservative Party.

**1979**
Became the first female prime minister of the UK.

**1990**
Resigned as prime minister and leader of the Conservative party.

**2008**
Presented with a lifetime achievement award by Prime Minister, David Cameron.

**2013**
Died in London, UK.

# Edith Wharton

Edith Wharton is one of America's most famous writers and the first woman to win the Pulitzer Prize for Literature. She wrote novels, plays, and short stories about the life of the aristocracy in the Gilded Age of the 1870s to 1900s.

Women in the wealthy New York society that Edith was born into were not expected to do anything beyond make a good marriage match. When Edith chose to become a writer it was quite shocking—but she went on to write forty books over forty years to great acclaim.

Edith spent the first ten years of her life traveling around Europe with her parents and two older brothers. She was exposed to art, architecture, and literature. As a child, her parents restricted what novels Edith was allowed to read. She read widely beyond the novel, making her way through the philosophy, history, poetry, and classic books in her father's library.

Edith "came out" in society when she was seventeen. This meant she was allowed to attend formal social occasions with the aim of finding a husband. She didn't marry her husband, Edward Wharton, until she was twenty-three, which was considered old for those times. They bought some land, and Edith designed and built their

> "I am an incorrigible life-lover and life-wonderer and adventurer."

home, The Mount. Now that she was married, Edith was able to read as many novels as she wished! She went on to write some of her most famous books, including *The House of Mirth* and *Ethan Frome*, in her marital home.

But when her marriage broke down in 1913, Edith moved to France for the rest of her life. She arrived just in time for the outbreak of World War I—and stayed in Paris to do charitable and humanitarian work. With her wealth, she set up convalescent homes for tuberculosis sufferers and schools for children fleeing from war in Belgium.

**1862**
Born in New York, USA.

**1885**
Married Edward Wharton.

**1905**
The House of Mirth published.

**1911**
Ethan Frome published.

**1921**
Won Pulitzer Prize for Literature for The Age of Innocence.

**1937**
Died in Saint-Brice-sous-Forêt, France.

# Jane Austen

Jane Austen is one of the most popular writers in British history. Jane was born in an English countryside village in 1775. She had one sister, Cassandra, and six brothers. The boys could all do exciting things like riding horses, and getting a good education, while Jane and Cassandra—like all girls at that time—were limited to activities such as sewing, singing, and housework. Jane thought that was boring and unfair.

Luckily, Jane's father ran a small boarding school for boys, and he was able to share the same books and lessons with Jane and Cassandra. Jane always loved reading and was more likely to be found reading in her father's library than playing with dolls.

Jane and her siblings would put on plays, often adapted from famous comedies, which influenced Jane in writing the satire that she became famous for. As a teenager, she wrote three short plays, and plenty of poems and stories that she would read aloud to entertain her family in the evenings. Her family enjoyed Jane's funny, anarchic tales where women held power. Jane realized that she wanted to become a writer herself and, as she became an adult, decided to write longer, more serious works that she could sell for money.

When Jane was twenty, she met a young man named Tom Lefroy, and they fell in love. However, his family forbade their marriage, as she was not rich. Jane channeled her heartbreak into her writing. *Pride and Prejudice* follows a storyline inspired by Jane and Tom, but she gave it a happy ending. *Pride and Prejudice* remains a hugely popular book today, because readers still identify with its daring heroine Lizzy, even though the times it was written in were very different from now.

Jane published six novels, and they all featured young women who were brave enough to make their own choices and never give up.

**1775**
Born in Hampshire, UK.

**1803**
Sold first novel, Northanger Abbey, but it wasn't published.

**1811**
Published Sense and Sensibility.

**1813**
Published Pride and Prejudice.

**1814**
Published Mansfield Park.

**1815**
Published Emma.

**1817**
Died in Winchester, UK.

**1817**
Persuasion and Northanger Abbey are published posthumously.

# Maya Angelou

Maya Angelou was an American writer and civil rights activist, who wrote about her life in her groundbreaking autobiographical books.

Maya was born in St. Louis, in 1928. When she was three years old her parents separated, and her father sent her and her four-year-old brother alone on a train to live with their grandmother in Arkansas.

Aged seven, she went to live with her mother, where a terrible incident transformed her life. Her mother's boyfriend, Freeman, abused her and Maya spoke out. Freeman was arrested and jailed—but only for one day. Soon after his release, he was murdered by Maya's uncles. The power of Maya's voice, that naming Freeman had led to his murder, caused her to become mute. She did not speak again for five years.

Mute, Maya developed an extraordinary memory and power of observation. She fell in love with books, and a teacher helped her find her voice again by introducing her to authors such as Dickens and Shakespeare.

Maya spent her teenage years with her mother in California. At sixteen, she became the first black female conductor on the San Francisco cable cars, a job she worked hard to get because she admired the uniforms. She completed school at seventeen and shortly afterward gave birth to her son.

She became a professional dancer, and changed her name from Marguerite Johnson to Maya Angelou. "Maya" was her brother's nickname for her, from "mya sister," and "Angelou" was her married name from her first husband. She toured Europe in a production of *Porgy and Bess* and used her observation and memory to learn the language of each country she visited.

Moving to New York City, Maya joined the Harlem Writers Guild, where she met famous African American authors of the time as well as the civil rights leader Martin Luther King, Jr. Her writing took her to Cairo, Egypt, and then Accra, Ghana, as a journalist, where she became friends with Malcolm X. She returned to the United States to help him build a civil rights organization, but he was assassinated shortly afterward.

Encouraged by her writing community, she wrote her first autobiography, *I Know Why the Caged Bird Sings*—an immediate bestseller. Maya wrote seven autobiographies and her last, *Mom & Me & Mom*, was published when she was eighty-five. In her writing, Maya retold her traumatic memories because she believed that telling "the human truth" was vital in allowing readers to forgive themselves.

When she died in 2014, President Obama called her "one of the brightest lights of our time."

**1928**
Born in St. Louis, Missouri, USA.

**1962**
Moved to Accra and met Malcolm X.

**1964**
Helped to set up the Organization of Afro-American Unity.

**1969**
Published first autobiographical novel, *I Know why the Caged Bird Sings*.

"If you are always trying to be normal, you will never know how amazing you can be."

**1982**
Became a Professor of American Studies at Wake Forest University

**2002**
A Song Flung Up to Heaven published.

**2011**
Received the Presidential Medal of Freedom.

**2013**
Mom & Me & Mom published.

**2014**
Died in North Carolina, USA.

19

# Toni Morrison

Toni Morrison is a multi-award-winning American writer. Her book *Beloved* won the Pulitzer Prize and was turned into a film starring Oprah Winfrey.

Toni was born in Lorain, Ohio, a racially diverse town her parents had moved to in order to escape the violent racism they had witnessed in Georgia and Alabama. When Toni was about two, her family couldn't afford to pay the rent, so their landlord set fire to their building while they were in it. They survived, and Toni learned from her parents that even when inexplicably bad things happen, laughter is a better choice than despair.

Toni read a lot as a child, and her parents shared African American folklore with her and her siblings. She graduated from Cornell University with a Master of Arts degree and taught English there before becoming an editor. She married, then divorced while she was pregnant with her second son. She raised both her children as a single mother working full-time. Toni wrote her first novel, *The Bluest Eye*, by getting up at four each morning before work.

Toni became the first black woman to be a senior fiction editor at New York City publisher Random House. She published black authors, bringing them to a wider audience, including now-famous names such as Chinua Achebe. She also compiled *The Black Book*, an anthology documenting black life in the USA from the time of slavery to the 1970s. This collection inspired her to write her best-known novel, *Beloved*.

She continued to write books and win awards through the 1970s, while working full-time as an editor. In 1983 she left publishing to spend her time writing and teaching.

When *Beloved* was published in 1987, it was a bestseller for twenty-five weeks and was celebrated by critics. It won the Pulitzer Prize for fiction and Toni became the first black woman to be awarded the Nobel Prize for Literature.

**1931**
Born in Lorain, Ohio, USA.

**1955**
Earned her Master of Arts degree from Cornell University, NY.

**1970**
*The Bluest Eye* was published.

**1987**
*Beloved* was published.

**1993**
Awarded the Nobel Prize for Literature.

**2012**
Awarded the Presidential Medal of Freedom.

# Patricia Bath

Patricia Bath was an American ophthalmologist (eye doctor) and inventor, who founded the American Institute for the Prevention of Blindness.

Patricia was born in Harlem, New York to parents who encouraged her education and love of culture. At school she did well in science and math and won a National Science Foundation scholarship to research the link between cancer, nutrition, and stress. Her findings were published in a scientific paper, and *Mademoiselle* magazine gave her a merit award for her contribution. She was still only eighteen years old.

After her degree in chemistry, Patricia went on to study medicine in Washington, D.C., and cofounded the Student National Medical Association, becoming its first woman president.

When civil rights leader Martin Luther King, Jr. was assassinated in 1968, Patricia chose to dedicate her work to his Poor People's Campaign. Columbia University gave her a one-year fellowship to research eye care at Harlem Hospital Center, where there was no ophthalmologist. Patricia's data showed that at Harlem there were far more cases of blindness than at Columbia University Eye Clinic. Her work convinced professors from Columbia to operate on patients at Harlem Hospital for free, and Patricia was one of the team to first perform eye surgery there.

Patricia's research showed that blindness was more common in black people. She pioneered "community ophthalmology," which promoted eye health in areas with less access to care.

Patricia became the first black resident eye doctor at New York University, then moved to Los Angeles and became the first woman eye doctor at UCLA. There she developed an innovative treatment to restore sight to some blind patients.

In 1986 she left Los Angeles to do research in laboratories in France, England, and Germany, following her love for different cultures.

In her career, Patricia invented four tools for helping eye surgery and became the first black American woman to hold a patent for a medical invention. Her work has restored sight to blind patients all over the world.

# Rosalind Franklin

Rosalind Franklin was a British chemist whose work in x-ray crystallography was pivotal in discovering the structure of DNA. This discovery revolutionized our understanding of life, medicine, and evolution.

Rosalind was born in 1920 in London to a wealthy Jewish family. She had a privileged education, and her intelligence was evident from a young age. Her aunt remarked that Rosalind spent all her time doing math for pleasure and always got her answers right. She went to St. Paul's School for Girls—one of few schools where girls could study physics and chemistry. She was usually top of her class, and she left school in 1938 with a scholarship to college. Her father asked her to give her scholarship to a refugee student, which she did. Her family helped to settle several Jewish children fleeing Nazi Europe into new homes, including their own.

Studying chemistry at Cambridge, Rosalind met Adrienne Weill, a French refugee who had studied with Marie Curie. She was an inspiration to Rosalind, and helped improve her French—which came in handy when she moved to Paris to work in a research lab.

In Paris, Rosalind used x-ray to study the structure of carbon and was respected for her intellect. After four years she moved to Kings College London, where she would be the only researcher with experience in these experimental techniques. She was recruited to work on the 3D structures of proteins but the head of the lab, John Randall, had her work on DNA molecules at the request of her colleague, Maurice Wilkins.

Rosalind put her all into her work, refining her skills in taking x-rays, and in 1951 she worked out some of DNA's key characteristics. She also discovered that DNA becomes long and thin when wet, and short and fat when dry.

Wilkins showed Rosalind's famous "Photo 51" of DNA to scientists James Watson and Francis Crick, who were also trying to uncover the structure of DNA. Photo 51 helped them figure out how to build a model.

In April 1953, Watson and Crick published their proposed model of DNA in the journal *Nature*, giving a short acknowledgment of the role of Franklin's and Wilkins's work.

Rosalind died in 1958 from ovarian cancer, possibly caused by all the x-rays she was exposed to in her research. Even while undergoing treatment, she continued working and publishing papers. In 1962 the Nobel Prize was awarded to Watson, Crick, and Wilkins for their work on DNA, but Rosalind was sadly overlooked. We are rewriting her into history today to acknowledge her outstanding contribution to modern science.

**1920**
Born in London, UK.

**1941**
Graduated from University of Cambridge.

**1945**
Earned her PhD in studies of coal.

**1951**
Became a research associate at King's College London.

"In my view, all that is necessary for faith is the belief that by doing our best we shall succeed in our aims: the improvement of mankind."

**1953**
Published her work on the structure of DNA.

**1953**
Moved to Birbeck College to study coal once more.

**1956**
Diagnosed with ovarian cancer.

**1958**
Died in London, UK.

**1962**
Watson, Crick, and Wilkins win the Nobel Prize for their work in DNA.

# Jane Goodall

Jane Goodall is a British primatologist whose study of chimpanzees furthered ideas of what it means to be human. She discovered that chimpanzees use tools—something previously thought to be unique to humans.

Growing up, Jane always wanted to work with wild animals, but her family didn't have enough money to send her to college. When a friend invited her to visit her in Kenya, Jane worked hard to afford the trip.

In Nairobi, Jane's friend encouraged her to meet with famous fossil expert Louis Leakey. He offered Jane a job—as his secretary. But he soon realized how serious she was about working with primates. He sent her to Gombe Stream National Park in Tanzania to study the chimpanzees.

Jane loved the freedom of working outdoors, climbing mountains, and watching the animals. The chimpanzees paid her no attention as she observed them every day. Jane was controversial among scientists because she wasn't qualified and didn't follow usual practices. She gave the chimpanzees names instead of referring to them by numbers and allowed them to become familiar with her.

Within two months, she had witnessed the chimpanzees eating meat and using sticks as tools to fish for termites. She even saw the chimpanzees perform what Jane called a "rain dance" during a thunderstorm. No one had seen these behaviors before, and it changed our perspective on humanity.

Louis Leakey even secured a place for Jane at the University of Cambridge to study for a PhD in ethology.

Jane learned from observing chimpanzee behavior that humans and chimps have much in common—individual personalities, emotions, kissing, hugging, and tickling. When she had her own child in 1967, she took mothering lessons from Flo, one of the best mothers in the troop.

In 1977, Jane set up the Jane Goodall Institute to support the research in Gombe. Now she travels the world advocating for conservation for chimpanzees.

**1934**
Born in London, UK.

**1960**
Arrived in Gombe Stream National Park.

**1963**
Published My Life Among the Wild Chimpanzees.

**1966**
Earned PhD from University of Cambridge.

**1977**
Jane Goodall Institute established.

**2002**
Jane was named a UN Messenger of Peace.

# Ada Lovelace

Ada Lovelace had a very privileged start to her life, but she defied the norms of her times to pursue her interest and talents in mathematics and science—including inventing the idea of computer programming—as far as she could as a woman of the Victorian era.

Ada's father was poet Lord Byron. He left his wife a month after Ada was born, and died when Ada was eight years old. Ada's mother wanted to ensure Ada didn't turn out like her father, so she encouraged her interest in mathematics and logic—which was unknown for girls in those days. In childhood, Ada was often ill, and measles left her paralyzed in bed for a year, with time to think and dream.

Deciding she wanted to fly, teenage Ada spent some years investigating how she could: studying the anatomy of birds and making her own wings from paper, silk, wire, and feathers. She wrote a book, *Flyology*, about her findings.

As a young woman, she met Charles Babbage, a professor of mathematics at Cambridge University, and heard about his plans for the "analytical engine"—a machine for making sophisticated calculations. Ada wrote her own work called *Sketch of Charles Babbage's Analytical Engine*, where she explained how it would work and even corrected some of the errors Babbage had made.

But it was also in *Sketch* that Ada made a leap of understanding that showed her to be a visionary of science and decades before her time. She foresaw how computers could do more than just complicated mathematical calculations—they could even be programmed to handle all sorts of tasks, such as composing music. She realized that any information could be converted to numbers—from the alphabet and language, to music and pictures—and therefore processed by a computer. But it wouldn't be until the late twentieth century that such things became possible, and in her time her work remained purely theoretical.

Her achievements—and those of all women in the fields of science, technology, engineering, and math—are commemorated on Ada Lovelace Day each year, on the second Tuesday of October.

**1815**
Born in London, UK.

**1829**
Suffered from measles.

**1833**
Met Charles Babbage, "the father of computers."

**1840**
Babbage delivered a lecture on his invention—the "analytical machine."

**1843**
Wrote the first algorithm in her notes on the translation of Babbage's lecture.

**1852**
Died in London, UK.

# Florence Griffith Joyner

Florence Griffith Joyner was an American athlete and the fastest woman on land—the records she set in 1988 haven't been beaten. She was also known for her personal style. Her flowing hair, colorful fingernails, and customized running suits made her stand out on the racetrack.

Florence was born in Los Angeles with ten brothers and sisters. She was athletic from a young age, and as a teenager she won the national youth games two years in a row. She was always interested in fashion and in high school she persuaded her track team to wear tights with their uniforms. She set new high school records in sprinting and long jump.

Florence went to college, and joined the track team where she flourished. She left briefly to get a job in a bank to support her family, but her college coach, recognizing her talent, fought to find her financial aid. She returned to college and qualified for the 1980 Olympics, but didn't compete because the USA boycotted the Olympics that year.

Her first Olympic games was in her hometown of Los Angeles four years later, where she won a silver medal for the 200 m. Afterward she briefly stopped running and worked again in a bank. When she married, her husband Al Joyner helped to coach her, and she returned to athletics in 1987. She broke the world record for 100 m in her trial for the 1988 Olympic games.

Florence became known as Flo-Jo. Her name and her looks made her memorable to audiences—but her speed bought her a place in history. She set the 200 m world record of 21.56 seconds. She won three gold medals and one silver—the second highest amount of Olympic medals won by a woman since 1948.

Flo-Jo retired from athletics and used her fame to endorse products, including a doll of herself. She died in her sleep aged thirty-eight but she still holds the world record for the fastest woman.

**1959**
Born in Los Angeles, California, USA.

**1983**
Graduated from UCLA with a degree in psychology.

**1984**
Won a silver medal at the Los Angeles Olympics.

**1988**
Broke the 100 m and 200 m world records at the Seoul Olympics.

**1998**
Died in California, USA.

# Simone Biles

Simone Biles is a champion gymnast. She has won more awards than any other American gymnast and has set so many medal-winning records that people consider her the greatest gymnast of all time.

Simone's early life was difficult. Her father was never around and her mother struggled with addictions, so Simone and her three siblings lived in foster homes. When her grandparents heard about this, they took care of the children and went on to adopt Simone and her younger sister, Adria.

Simone was always energetic. It was on a group trip, aged six, that she got her first taste of gymnastics. The fearlessness, coordination, and strength she showed that day impressed the instructor, who suggested that she continue with it. Strength and power came easily to Simone, but she had to work hard to learn how to control her power, become more flexible, and put her body into the right shapes when leaping and jumping.

Simone trained for twenty hours a week—four hours a day, five days a week, on top of school hours. The hard work paid off, and when she was fifteen she made the US national team. Then Simone decided to be home-schooled so she could spend more time training. Putting in more hours soon brought results; she came in first and second in international competitions.

However, the stress of huge expectations at just sixteen years old made Simone doubt herself and begin to make mistakes. A sports psychologist helped her to deal with her stress, and that year she went on to win three of her world titles. Knowing when to pull back from intensive training has helped Simone stay healthy. After winning four gold medals at the 2016 Rio Olympics, she chose to take a year off from competing and wrote her memoir, called *Courage to Soar*. At Rio she did a double layout with a half twist, a move that had never been seen before and has been named "the Biles."

**1997**
Born in Columbus, Ohio, USA.

**2003**
Adopted by her grandparents.

**2012**
Selected for the USA Gymnastics National Championships.

**2015**
Graduated from school.

**2016**
Competed in the Rio Olympics.

**2017**
Took a year off competing to write her memoir.

**2018**
Returned to competitive gymnastics.

# Althea Gibson

Althea Gibson is considered one of the greatest tennis players of all time. She was the first African American to win a Grand Slam title, winning eleven over the course of her career. Not only did she have an impressive career, but also it was all the more extraordinary that her success came at a time of widespread racism in sport and society.

Althea was born on her parents' cotton farm in South Carolina, but during the Great Depression her parents moved to Harlem, New York. The city was a great place for Althea to start in tennis: her street was in a designated play area, meaning it was closed to traffic in daylight hours so children could play organized sports. She quickly became skilled at paddle tennis (a simple, informal version of tennis) and by the age of twelve became New York City women's champion.

As a teenager, Althea started winning national championships. She always had confidence in herself and was driven by wanting to prove her talent to her opponents. With mentorship and training, in 1949 she became the first black woman to play in the National Indoor Championships and was given a full athletics scholarship to study at Florida A&M University.

For a time she couldn't play in the US National Championships, despite rules officially prohibiting racial discrimination. To enter the competition, players must win a certain number of points—which could only be gained from playing at white-only clubs. But her talent was so obvious that officials lobbied for her to be specially invited to compete. In 1950 she was the first black player to set foot on those courts.

When she became the first black player to win at Wimbledon, in 1957, she remarked that shaking Queen Elizabeth II's hand was a long way from having to sit in the colored section of the bus.

In the fifties, tennis was not a professional sport, and Althea earned very little money. She tried singing, acting, and writing her memoir to earn more. As for tennis, she realized that although she had crossed so many racial barriers, they hadn't been completely knocked down—white men she had previously beaten were being given opportunities that she was denied.

In her late thirties, Althea took up professional golf, and did well, but segregation kept her from competing in the south, and in some places she wasn't even allowed to use the changing rooms.

After retiring from professional sports, Althea worked on projects bringing tennis equipment to underprivileged areas in large cities, and coached future tennis stars.

Venus and Serena Williams both cite Althea as a huge inspiration and acknowledge how her success paved the way for their success too.

**1927**
Born in Silver, South Carolina, USA.

**1930**
Moved to New York City.

**1939**
Became New York City women's paddle tennis champion.

**1950**
Was the first black player in US National Championships.

"I always wanted to be somebody. If I made it it's half because I was game enough to take a lot of punishment along the way and half because there were a lot of people who cared enough to help me."

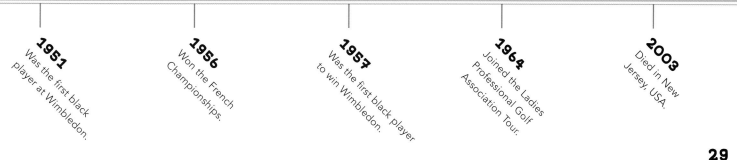

**1951**
Was the first black player at Wimbledon.

**1956**
Won the French Championships.

**1957**
Was the first black player to win Wimbledon.

**1964**
Joined the Ladies Professional Golf Association Tour.

**2003**
Died in New Jersey, USA.

# Michelle Kwan

M ichelle Kwan is an American figure skater, who has won the most medals in US history, and is considered one of the greatest ice skaters of all time.

Michelle was born in California to parents from Hong Kong, and she grew up speaking both Cantonese and English. She started ice skating when she was just five years old. She and her sister Karen trained at five o'clock each morning and then again after school. By the time Michelle was ten, her family couldn't afford to pay for their training, but someone at the Los Angeles Figure Skating Club offered Michelle financial assistance.

By age eleven, Michelle was competing in national competitions, and she won the World Junior Championships when she was thirteen.

The same year she went on the US team to the winter Olympics in Lillehammer as a reserve, but didn't compete.

For the next few years Michelle competed and improved, placing high but not quite making gold medal status. She developed a more mature, expressive style of performing, and in 1998, despite a fractured toe, she won the US National Championship, and won silver at the winter Olympics in Nagano, Japan.

Michelle competed for the last time at the 2005 World Championship, which was the first time she failed to win any medal at an international competition since 1995.

In 2006 Michelle became a public diplomacy advisor, and she enjoyed traveling the world representing American values to young people and sports enthusiasts. In 2009 she graduated from the University of Denver in international studies and decided that her future lay in further education and diplomacy. In 2012 she was appointed a senior advisor for public diplomacy and public affairs to the US State Department.

**1980**
Born in Torrance, California, USA.

**1998**
Won the Silver at the Nagano Winter Olympics.

**2001**
Awarded the James E. Sullivan Award for America's best amateur athlete.

**2005**
Competed for the final time.

**2009**
Graduated from the University of Denver.

**2012**
Appointed a senior advisor for public diplomacy and public affairs.

# Harriet Tubman

Harriet Tubman was one of the most courageous women in American history. She was born into slavery and escaped it, risking her life many times to save others.

As a child, Harriet was called Minty. When she was six, Minty was taken away from her parents to work on a different plantation, where she was whipped and beaten daily. One day, an iron weight hit her on the head. She was unconscious for two days and suffered from headaches and narcolepsy (sleeping spells) for the rest of her life.

Her narcolepsy meant no other plantation owner would buy her, so she was put to work with her father, chopping wood. She grew strong from the work and also met free black workers, who shipped the wood north where slavery was forbidden. She married one of these free men, John Tubman, and changed her name to Harriet, to help disguise her.

When she was twenty-seven, Harriet escaped, and followed the North Star to lead her to freedom in Pennsylvania. She had learned from

hundreds of others escape. In 1863, during the Civil War, she was the first woman in US history to plan and lead a military raid, freeing 750 slaves from South Carolina.

The Civil War abolished slavery and gave rights to many freed slaves—but women were still not allowed to vote. Harriet joined the fight for female suffrage. She had to fight for a pension for her army work—and was finally granted $20 a month. In 2016, the US Treasury decided to commemorate Harriet Tubman by putting her face on $20 notes.

*"Always remember, you have within you the strength, the patience, and the passion to reach for the stars to change the world."*

the free black workers about a network of safe houses, and boat and cart drivers who helped slaves to escape.

She thought the north was wonderful, but was unable to enjoy her freedom while so many of her loved ones were still enslaved. So she returned to the south thirteen times to help her relatives and

**1822**
Born in Dorchester County, Maryland, USA.

**1844**
Married John Tubman.

**1849**
Escaped to Philadelphia.

**1861**
Civil War broke out.

**1863**
Rescued 750 slaves in a military raid in South Carolina.

**1913**
Died in New York, USA.

# Rosa Parks

Rosa Parks was a leading figure in the American civil rights movement. She is most famous for a simple act of defiance, for which the US Congress honored her as "the mother of the freedom movement."

Rosa Parks lived in Montgomery, Alabama during a time of enforced racial segregation, including in public transportation. Black people were expected to sit at the back of the public buses, while whites sat at the front. The majority of people using public buses in Montgomery were black. But all bus drivers were white, and they enforced segregation laws, often in a cruel manner. In 1943, a bus driver ordered Mrs. Parks to be removed from a bus because she had boarded at the front door. It did not matter that she could not board at the back door because the bus was overcrowded.

Rosa Parks had a job as a seamstress, but she was also a secretary in the local office of the National Association for the Advancement of Colored People (NAACP). Here she helped investigate crimes against black people. She attended a mass meeting about the killings of two black activists and a young black teenager, Emmett Till—whose murderers had recently been acquitted.

This injustice led Mrs. Parks to believe that she and others had to do more to end racial segregation. Later that year, on December 1st, Mrs. Parks was seated in the "black section" of a bus when the bus driver ordered her and three others in her row to give up their seats for one white passenger. The other passengers protested, but ultimately complied. Rosa Parks refused.

The bus driver called the police and she was arrested. She was not the first person to be arrested for refusing to give up her seat, but she was committed to standing up for her equal rights before the law. Mrs. Parks prepared for a tough fight, risking her life in order to combat segration.

In support, black residents of Montgomery, led by Martin Luther King Jr., boycotted the city's buses for 381 days. Across the country pressure grew so strong that the US Supreme Court ruled that Montgomery's segregation laws were illegal.

Rosa's strength of character and endurance enabled this campaign and victory, but as she acknowledged in her autobiography, there is still a long way to go before black and white people are truly equal. Yet she paved a lot of the way herself, and when she died she lay in honor in the US Capitol building—the first American who had not been a government official to do so.

**1913**
Born in Tuskegee, Alabama, USA.

**1932**
Married Raymond Parks.

**1933**
Completed her high school certificate.

**1943**
Joined NAACP.

"I have learned over the years that when one's mind is made up, this diminishes fear."

**1955**
Refused to give up her seat on the bus.

**1956**
The Montgomery buses were desegregated.

**1992**
Published her first book, Rosa Parks, My Story.

**1996**
Received the Medal of Freedom from President Bill Clinton.

**2005**
Died in Detroit, Michigan, USA.

**33**

# Malala Yousafzai

Malala Yousafzai is a Pakistani activist for female education and the youngest ever Nobel laureate.

Malala was born in the Swat area of Pakistan. Her family ran schools but, because she was a girl, Malala was only allowed a basic education. She had two strong role models though: Benazir Bhutto, Pakistan's female prime minister, and her father, Ziauddin, who supported female education.

When Malala was eleven, the Taliban took control of her town and banned television and music. They even banned girls from going to school. As these changes were happening, Malala blogged for the BBC under a secret name. This was her first taste of sharing her views on freedom and education. As fighting began, she was sent to live with family in the countryside, while her father went to Peshawar to lobby for support. Malala had always dreamed of becoming a doctor but, inspired by her father, she instead decided to become a politician.

When Malala and her family returned home, she began to speak out on television and radio about female education. She was awarded Pakistan's first National Youth Peace Prize. The government named a secondary school after her and set up an IT campus at her local women's college in her honor.

The more famous she became, the more she was threatened by the Taliban until, when she was fifteen, the threats became real. She was riding the bus home after an exam at school, when a masked gunman boarded the bus and asked, "Who is Malala?" before shooting her in the head.

She was given a 70 percent chance of survival. A few days later she flew to Birmingham, UK, for specialist treatment. After months of surgery and therapies, Malala recovered. She has dedicated her second chance at life to fighting for every girl's right to education.

She set up the Malala Fund, a charity for improving girls' life chances. This includes a school for Syrian refugees in Lebanon, and calling on world leaders to fund "books, not bullets."

**1997**
Born in Swat, Pakistan.

**2008**
Started blogging for BBC Urdu.

**2011**
Awarded Pakistan's National Youth Peace Prize.

**2012**
Shot by the Taliban.

**2013**
I Am Malala published and and the Malala Fund was founded.

**2014**
Awarded the Nobel Peace Prize.

# Gloria Steinem

Gloria Steinem is an American journalist and activist whose writings since the 1960s have exposed inequalities in the way society treats men and women. Today, she works to increase the visibility of women in the media.

Gloria spent her early years traveling with her parents in their trailer. Her father was an antiques dealer and never liked to stay in one place for long. This meant that she didn't go to school until she was twelve years old. But with the help of librarians, she read a book a day. Being left to think for herself in these early years gave Gloria a different outlook from most other children.

Gloria's mother had had a nervous breakdown before Gloria was born, and when her parents separated in 1944, Gloria took care of her. As a child Gloria thought her mother was mad,

> "If it's not good for all women, it's not good for any living thing."

because that's what the doctors said, and she worried it was something she might inherit. But Gloria's independent thinking helped her to realize that her mother's illness was misdiagnosed. She was depressed and had become addicted to the medication wrongly prescribed to her. Gloria saw her mother's situation as an example of how women didn't have an equal standing with men in society.

After graduating from college, Gloria worked in India before becoming a journalist in New York City. In 1963 she became famous for writing an eye-opening exposé of the Playboy Mansion.

She went undercover and spent eleven days working as a Playboy Bunny, documenting the sexist treatment she experienced there.

In 1972 Gloria was one of the founding editors of a new feminist magazine, *Ms.*, which published feminist articles instead of the usual recipes and domestic tips found in other women's magazines.

Today, when Gloria is invited to give a speech, she only accepts if there is also a woman of color on the same program. Aware that new elements of feminism need to be fought for, she now uses her position to help raise other feminist issues in society such as race and class.

**1934**
Born in Toledo, Ohio, USA.

**1944**
Her parents separated.

**1963**
Published her Playboy Mansion exposé.

**1972**
Cofounded Ms. magazine.

**2005**
Cofounded the Women's Media Center.

**2013**
Awarded the Presidential Medal of Freedom.

# Mary Wollstonecraft

Mary Wollstonecraft was an English writer and philosopher. Her book *A Vindication of the Rights of Woman* became an influence on future feminist thinking.

Mary was the second of seven children of a wealthy family. However, as she grew up her father lost their money and the family became poor and unstable. She became aware of injustice in society, as her father could be violent. Mary tried to protect her mother from his rages. Eager to leave home as soon as she was able, Mary took a job as a "lady's companion" in Bath. She returned to London to care for her mother when she became ill.

When her mother died, Mary didn't want to go back to Bath and so, with her sisters and best friend, she set up a girl's boarding school and lived in a community of Dissenters—people who rejected the standard Church of England philosophy.

In the late eighteenth century there were very strict rules for how women should behave. Mary never felt she had to follow these rules if another way seemed better. In her book, she argued against marriage. So when she fell in love with an American adventurer, Gilbert Imlay, they had a daughter despite not being married—this was unheard of for a respectable woman. She and her daughter accompanied him on perilous journeys through Revolutionary France and to Scandinavia. But her relationship with Gilbert broke down and, returning to England, Mary became suicidal.

Later, through her publishing Mary met the love of her life, William Godwin, and again became pregnant. This time she married, but eleven days after giving birth to her daughter, Mary died of blood poisoning. Godwin was heartbroken.

For a long time, Mary was best known for her unconventional life but more recently she is celebrated for her arguments for gender equality. Mary's second daughter grew up to be Mary Shelley, the author of *Frankenstein*.

**1759**
Born in London, UK.

**1784**
Opened a girl's boarding school.

**1788**
Published her children's book, *Original Stories from Real Life*.

**1792**
Published *A Vindication of the Rights of Women*.

**1794**
Gave birth to her daughter Fanny in Paris.

**1797**
Gave birth to her daughter Mary in London.

**1797**
Died in London, UK.

# Ruth Bader Ginsburg

Ruth Bader Ginsburg is one of only four women ever to serve on the Supreme Court of the United States. Throughout her legal career she has made huge gains for gender equality and women's rights.

Born in New York in 1933, her mother Celia encouraged Ruth's education because she hadn't been able to study further than high school herself. Celia sadly died of cancer the day before Ruth graduated from high school, so she never witnessed just how much more her daughter went on to achieve.

Ruth graduated from Cornell University with a degree in government as the highest-ranking woman in her class. She married Martin Ginsburg, and when she got pregnant she was demoted from her administration job—an experience that would fuel her later work.

Both Ruth and Martin enrolled at Harvard Law School. Ruth was one of only nine women in a class of 500—a professor even asked why she was there, taking the place of a man. Soon after, Martin was diagnosed with cancer. Ruth cared for him and her daughter, while also attending both her classes and Martin's.

Ruth transferred to Columbia University in New York, where she graduated joint-first in her class. Despite her stellar reputation, in the late 1950s women were considered too emotional to be lawyers. The only job she could get was teaching in a college.

Ruth cofounded the Women's Rights Project at the American Civil Liberties Union, which took on cases of gender discrimination. As a highly-intelligent woman with an understanding of the workings of the male-dominated legal system, Ruth chose clever ways to appeal to the courts. Each case she brought, she showed how gender discrimination affected men as well as women. The courts found those examples easier to understand, and she won many cases that slowly removed gender discrimination from the law.

In 1993, President Bill Clinton nominated her as the second-ever female Associate Justice of the Supreme Court. She continues to fight for gender equality, rarely missing a day's work even when undergoing treatment for cancer.

**1933**
Born in Brooklyn, New York, USA.

**1954**
Graduated from Cornell University.

**1956**
Enrolled at Harvard University.

**1959**
Graduated in joint-first place from Columbia University.

**1993**
Appointed as Associate Justice of the Supreme Court.

**2002**
Inducted into the National Women's Hall of Fame.

# Florence Nightingale

Florence Nightingale was an English nurse who changed the perception of the profession and set up the first nursing training school. She not only cared for the wounded and ill, but developed research into important guidelines for patient care.

Florence was named after the Italian city, where she was born to wealthy English parents. They moved back to England the following year, and Florence grew up in Hampshire and Derbyshire.

Women of Florence's position in society were only expected to marry well, not to work. However, as a child Florence excelled in her studies and when she was seventeen she felt a "calling" from God to devote her life to the service of others.

In those days, nursing had a poor reputation and was not an acceptable occupation for affluent women. But Florence educated herself and persuaded her parents to let her study nursing in Dusseldorf. She then got a job as a superintendent at a hospital for gentlewomen in Harley Street, London.

In 1854 Florence took thirty-eight nurses whom she had trained to Turkey to care for soldiers wounded in the Crimean War. Florence recorded that ten times more soldiers died from diseases such as typhus, cholera, and dysentery than from battle wounds. She improved the basic hygiene practices in the hospital and the death rate dropped from 42 percent to just 2 percent of soldiers. She became famous for her nightly checks on the soldiers—the sight of "the Lady with the Lamp" brought comfort to many.

Florence believed that the death rate was high due to the poor sanitation, lack of fresh air and medical supplies, and overworking the soldiers. She collected evidence to back up her claims and vividly communicated the results of her research in graphics—including the pie chart, which she invented. She was hailed as a hero for her work in the Crimean War, and her messages of sanitation advice inspired people to donate money to the Nightingale Fund.

Florence used money from the Nightingale Fund to set up the world's first nursing training school, at St. Thomas' Hospital. She wrote *Notes on Nursing*, a book that was used in the Nightingale Training School. Florence had turned around nursing's reputation to a respectable career for women.

Florence met Queen Victoria and they corresponded over many years, so even as she got older and was often confined to her sick bed, Florence continued to influence the highest levels of British society. The International Nurses Day was set up to celebrate nurses around the world on May 12—Florence's birthday.

**1820**
Born in Florence, Tuscany.

**1853**
Became Superintendent at a hospital for gentlewomen in Harley Street, London.

**1854**
Nursed wounded soldiers in the Crimean War.

**1859**
Wrote Notes on Nursing.

"I attribute my success to this— I never gave or took any excuse."

**1860**
Set up the Nightingale training school.

**1883**
Awarded the Royal Red Cross.

**1907**
Received the Order of Merit.

**1909**
Awarded the Freedom of the City of London.

**1910**
Died in London, UK.

# Katharine Graham

Katharine Graham was an American newspaper publisher who headed up *The Washington Post* for more than twenty years. She oversaw the publication of information that led to the resignation of president Richard Nixon.

Katharine's family was very wealthy. Growing up, she and her four siblings moved between their estate in New York and a mansion in Washington, D.C. She wasn't close with her parents—they were often traveling and socializing and her mother was not always kind to Katharine, which damaged her self-confidence.

When Katharine was a teenager in 1933, the newspaper *The Washington Post* went bankrupt. Her father, Eugene, bought the paper and returned it to financial health and respectability.

In 1946 Eugene left *The Washington Post* and made Katharine's husband, Philip Graham, publisher. Katharine's marriage hadn't always been happy, as Philip had mood swings and—like her mother—would belittle her. He had

been preparing to divorce Katharine when he died suddenly in 1963. Katharine became the newspaper's publisher, and she flourished as its well-respected figurehead.

At first, Katharine doubted her own knowledge and confidence. There were no female CEOs in any of the other top-500 American companies to guide her. She was leading the field by herself. However, the growing women's movement in the late 1960s helped Katharine develop a confident attitude and encouraged her to promote gender equality throughout the company.

In the early 1970s, President Nixon was involved in the Watergate scandal. It was thanks to two reporters at *The Washington Post* whose investigative journalism uncovered the most damning details that Nixon eventually resigned. Katharine supported her editor and journalists in publishing this evidence, even when she received personal threats from the attorney general. The *Post's* reputation soared and in 1974, applications to study journalism reached an all-time high.

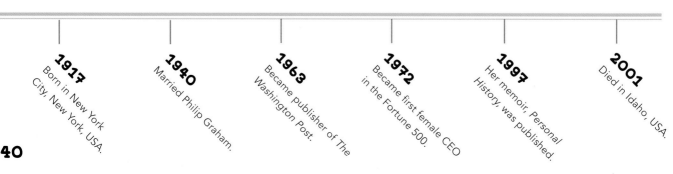

**1917**
Born in New York City, New York, USA.

**1940**
Married Philip Graham.

**1963**
Became publisher of The Washington Post.

**1972**
Became first female CEO in the Fortune 500.

**1997**
Her memoir, *Personal History*, was published.

**2001**
Died in Idaho, USA.

# Madonna

Madonna is an American singer and actress who has repeatedly reinvented her style since the 1980s. She has influenced many of today's female pop icons.

Madonna grew up in Detroit with five siblings. When she was five, her mother died suddenly of breast cancer. Madonna did well in school because she knew that without her mother around she had to take care of herself. She was unconventional, cartwheeling in school corridors and choosing not to wear makeup.

When Madonna was twenty, she moved to New York City with only $35 in her pocket. It was the bravest thing she had ever done. After performing in rock bands, she signed a record deal. Her third single, "*Holiday*," was an international hit, and her style—lacy tops, fishnet stockings, and bleached hair—was as iconic as her music.

In 1984, "*Like a Virgin*" went to number one in America for six weeks. Madonna became famous for the song's controversy—some people thought it undermined traditional family values. Whatever Madonna did next, the media commented on it, but she never apologized for having her own opinions.

> "I don't accept injustice. And neither should you."

Madonna was quick to realize that a strong music video could win her fans who wouldn't be able to see her perform live. Her music videos are always novel, often telling a story alongside the music, or popularizing a new dance style.

Madonna's 1990 *Blond Ambition* world tour was an extravaganza of choreography, set design, and costume changes. Madonna was insecure about her vocal skills, so she made the show about much more than just her voice. Its scale changed expectations for music tours forever.

Through her career Madonna has acted in films with mixed reviews—but a bad reception never stopped her from trying. In 1996 she starred in *Evita*, the role she was most proud of.

Madonna champions diversity. Her videos includes dancers of many different backgrounds and, in the 1980s, the cover sleeve of her *Like a Prayer* album included health information about AIDS, a subject that was taboo at the time. As she grows older, she refuses to bow to society's expectations of how a woman should behave.

**1958**
Born in Bay City, Michigan, USA.

**1978**
Moved to New York City.

**1982**
Signed first record deal, with Sire Records.

**1983**
Released debut album, *Madonna.*

**1990**
Blond Ambition tour.

**2006**
Cofounded Raising Malawi Charity.

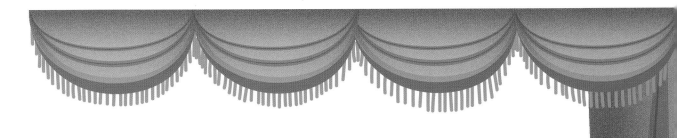

# Ella Fitzgerald ®

Ella Fitzgerald was an American jazz singer, known for her smooth voice and wide vocal range. A cultural ambassador, her art brought people together.

Born in the American South, Ella's parents split up when she was young. With her mother, Ella moved to Yonkers in New York. Many African Americans were moving north to find work and better race relations.

Ella did well in school. She loved dancing and entertained her friends during lunch hour. She first experienced music at church and loved to listen to her mother's jazz records. But when she was fifteen, her mother died in an accident and Ella's life started to fall apart. She skipped school and ran with a rough crowd. When she was caught, she was sent to reform school. She escaped and spent time homeless, surviving by singing on the streets of Harlem.

Ella tried her luck one night at the Apollo Theater's Amateur Night—a talent contest. She planned to dance but lost her nerve when she saw another troop's entry and sang instead, winning first prize of $25. The theater withheld part of her prize—the chance to perform there for a week—because she looked so unkempt from living on the streets.

The following year, Ella joined the *Chick Webb Orchestra*. Together they recorded several hit records and Ella's version of *A-Tisket A-Tasket* was one of the best-selling records of the 1930s.

Soon afterward, Chick Webb died and Ella took over as bandleader, renaming the group *Ella and Her Famous Orchestra*. But it wasn't until she became a solo singer in 1942 that her career really took off. A new style of jazz called bebop was becoming popular, and Ella developed a "scat" style of singing—wordless and improvised to mimic the sound of the horns.

In 1949, Ella was part of a tour that chose to perform at racially segregated venues, but insisted that the seating would be mixed—with no separate "whites only" section—and if the venue refused, the concert was canceled.

As bebop's popularity faded in the 1950s, Ella looked to reach an audience beyond jazz fans. She released an album of songs by Cole Porter, a popular composer of musicals from the 1920s and '30s. She recorded eight albums of songs by different composers, together called the *Great American Songbook*. These albums are her best known works. Her audience was as diverse as her vocal range and Ella's talent allowed her to pave the way for other African American performers.

Through the 1950s to 1970s she recorded and performed around the world, until she became too ill. In the 1990s, she founded a charity to give back to less fortunate people, remembering her own beginnings.

**1917**
Born in Newport News, Virginia, USA.

**1934**
Won the talent show at the Apollo Theater, Harlem.

**1935**
Joined the Chick Webb Orchestra.

"Just don't give up trying to do what you really want to do. Where there is love and inspiration, I don't think you can go wrong."

**1938**
Cowrote and released A-Tisket A-Tasket.

**1956**
Released Ella Fitzgerald Sings the Cole Porter Song Book.

**1987**
Received the National Medal of Arts.

**1993**
Founded the Ella Fitzgerald Charitable Foundation.

**1996**
Died in California, USA.

# Adele

Adele is one of the most successful singers in pop history. Her album *21*, which she wrote when she was only twenty-one years old, became the fourth best-selling album ever in the United Kingdom. Her voice is powerful, soulful, and distinctive, but it is the combination of her voice and her song-writing that makes her songs so popular.

Adele stands out in the pop world because she writes her own songs. Her lyrics are authentic in their emotion, and through writing honestly about her life as a young woman, she captures universal experiences that so many other people can identify with.

Adele grew up in London, living with just her mother, and she always loved to sing. She went to the famous BRIT school, a performing arts school in South London, though back then she imagined she would be launching other people's careers rather than singing herself.

Soon after leaving school, a record company found a demo of Adele singing her own songs that a friend had put on the internet, and over the next two years she wrote, recorded, and released an album, *19*, about her life as a nineteen-year-old. When *19* was released, it went straight to number one in the charts in the UK.

Her bestselling single is "*Hello*," which spent ten weeks at number one in the United States. Her song "*Skyfall*" was written for the James Bond film and won an Oscar for Best Original Song.

Apart from her music, Adele is popular because

> "I have insecurities of course, but I don't hang out with anyone who points them out to me."

of her down-to-earth personality and the fact that she is true to herself, speaking her mind but always with kindness and humor. She has been open about her experiences with panic attacks and postpartum depression, as she knows it can be very helpful for others going through the same thing to see it normalized and nothing to be ashamed of.

With her tours and records generating so much money, Adele has often performed for free at charity concerts, and asks people visiting her backstage to donate money to the Still Birth and Neonatal Death Society—one tour alone raised $13,000. After the Grenfell Tower fire in London in 2017, Adele joined the vigil and brought cakes for the firefighters.

**1988**
Born in London, UK.

**2006**
Graduated from the BRIT School.

**2008**
Her first album, *19*, was released.

**2011**
Her second album, *21*, was released.

**2013**
*Skyfall* won an Oscar for Best Original Song.

**2015**
Her third album, *25*, released.

# Aretha Franklin

Aretha Franklin was a soul singer, songwriter, and civil rights activist known as the "Queen of Soul." Her voice was powerful and full of strength and emotion. In 1987, she was the first female artist to be inducted into the Rock and Roll Hall of Fame, an archive of influential rock and roll musicians.

Aretha started singing gospel music in the Baptist church in Detroit where her father was minister. His sermons were famous for their passion and he was nicknamed the "million-dollar voice"—something that would become true of his daughter. Aretha's parents split up when she was six years old, and her mother moved away. They stayed in touch, but her mother died when Aretha was ten.

Aretha didn't complete high school, and when she was a young teenager she had two children, whom her grandmother and sister helped to raise. When she was growing up, she met many of her father's famous friends, including Martin Luther King, Jr. and musicians Clara Ward, Sam Cooke, and Jackie Wilson, who all became big influences on Aretha's dreams and ethics.

When she turned eighteen, she told her father she wanted to move to New York to become a pop singer, like Sam Cooke. Her father agreed to be her manager, but it was in 1966 when she moved record labels that she truly became a pop star. She recorded "*Respect,*" which became her signature song as well as an anthem for the feminist and civil rights movements.

From the influence of her father and home life, Aretha was for the rest of her life immersed in the movements for civil rights and women's rights. She also supported Native American rights. She provided financial support as well as performing at benefit concerts and speaking out.

When she died in August 2018, former US President Barack Obama said Aretha had "helped define the American experience," celebrating how in her music she blended songs of hardship and sorrow into "something full of beauty, vitality, and hope."

**1942**
Born in Memphis, Tennessee, USA.

**1956**
Released her first album of gospel songs recorded in her dad's church.

**1966**
Signed with Atlantic Records.

**1967**
Respect released.

**1979**
Received a star on the Hollywood Walk of Fame.

**1987**
Inducted to the Rock and Roll Hall of Fame.

**2018**
Died in Michigan, USA.

# Mae Jemison

ae Jemison is a NASA astronaut and the first African American woman to travel in space. She is a medical doctor and has nine honorary doctorates.

Mae grew up in Chicago, Illinois. As a child she assumed she would be able to travel in space but later realized that the only way to do it was as an astronaut. When the Apollo space program launched in 1968, Mae didn't understand why there were no female astronauts.

Mae loved science in school, but she also loved the arts, especially dancing, as a way to express herself. She attended Stanford University at the age of only sixteen, and graduated with a BSc in chemical engineering and a BA in African and Afro-American studies. In college, she experienced sexism and racism, but her strong belief in herself helped her excel.

She wasn't sure whether to study to be a doctor or a dancer. Her mother pointed out that doctors can dance, but dancers can't doctor. So, she studied hard at medical school and became a GP—all while taking dance lessons and even building her own dance studio.

Mae spent two years working as a doctor for the Peace Corps in Liberia and Sierra Leone. Her quick and assertive decision-making saved a volunteer's life, after she diagnosed him with meningitis and arranged his urgent evacuation.

Mae applied to NASA in 1983, inspired by Sally Ride, the first American woman in space, as well as the black actress Nichelle Nichols, who played Lt. Uhura on *Star Trek*. Mae was one of fifteen candidates chosen from 2,000 applicants. On her space mission she took a small statuette from West Africa, to symbolize how space belongs to all nations.

When Mae left NASA in 1993, it was to found her own company to develop science and technology for everyday life.

**1956**
Born in Decatur, Alabama, USA.

**1977**
Graduated from Stanford University.

**1981**
Qualified as a doctor from Cornell Medical School.

**1983–85**
Served as a medical officer in the Peace Corps.

**1987**
Joined NASA.

**1992**
Went into orbit on Space Shuttle Endeavour.

# Sacagawea

Sacagawea was a Native American woman of the Shoshone tribe, in the early nineteenth century. Life for Native American women could be hard—they had no independence and were viewed as the property of the tribe. Sacagawea suffered from this lack of freedom when, aged twelve, she was kidnapped by the Hidatsa tribe. Then a year or so later she was sold as a wife to French Canadian Toussaint Charbonneau, a hunter who lived in the village.

Soon after, her life altered once more when an expedition from the US Army arrived nearby. The Corps of Discovery, led by two men named Lewis and Clark, was exploring the Pacific Northwest. They asked Toussaint and Sacagawea to join the expedition because Sacagawea spoke Shoshone and could interpret for them along the way.

Although Sacagawea hadn't been able to make many of her own choices so far in life, being taken along on the expedition gave her a chance to prove her skills—and Lewis and Clark recognized that she was indispensable.

When they set off, Sacagawea had a newborn baby—her son, Jean Baptiste—whom she carried on her back for the whole journey. She was viewed as a good sign that the expedition party came in peace, and she helped them befriend the tribes they encountered by being able to speak their language.

Food was hard to come by, but Sacagawea knew how to forage for roots and berries and kept the party alive. The group had to cross treacherous landscapes, but Sacagawea found the best crossing point through the Rocky Mountains; later a railway was built there.

A month into the journey, a boat capsized and equipment and important journals would have been lost had Sacagawea not quickly rescued them. The commanders named the river after her in thanks. The adventure was tough for all, but made easier by Sacagawea's knowledge, skills, and kindness.

**1788**
Born near Salmon, Idaho, USA.

**1800**
Kidnapped by the Hidatsa tribe.

**1801**
Sold into marriage to Toussaint Charbonneau.

**1804**
Corps of Discovery arrived near the Hidatsa villages.

**1805**
Jean-Baptiste was born.

**1805**
Sacagawea left with Lewis and Clark on their expedition.

**1812**
Died in Missouri, USA.

# Amelia Earhart

Amelia Earhart was a pioneering aviator from when few people, and almost no women, flew planes. She disappeared during her attempt at flying around the whole world, and she is remembered most for her bravery and ambition.

Amelia was born in Atchison, Kansas, USA in 1897. She and her sister spent most of their childhood living with their grandparents, as their father struggled to find employment to be able to provide for his family. Whenever times were tough, their mother took them to their grandparents' upper-middle-class home. Amelia's grandmother disapproved of the bloomers (loose pants) she wore, because she thought girls should wear pretty dresses. But bloomers allowed Amelia the freedom to expore the neighborhood, hunting rats and climbing trees. While her father's inability to provide for his family toughened Amelia and shaped her independence, it was this spirit of adventure and refusal to behave as a "nice little girl" that ultimately led her to become the first woman to fly solo across the Atlantic.

Her first experience of flying was in 1918 when she saw an airplane display put on by a World War I pilot who had just returned to Canada. During the display he dived at Earhart and her friend, and Amelia was sure the plane had said something to her as it passed by.

When she was 23, she had a ten-minute ride in an airplane and that was when she knew she had to fly. She worked hard in all sorts of jobs, from truck driver to photographer, to save up the money to take flying lessons. After six months, Earhart bought her own bright yellow airplane, which she called *The Canary*, and she embarked on her life's mission of making a name for herself in aviation.

She quickly started breaking records. In 1922 she flew up to 14,000 feet, the world altitude record for a female pilot, and in 1923 she became the sixteenth American woman to be given a pilot's license. In 1928, she was the first woman to cross the Atlantic in a plane, but she became a true pioneer in 1932, when she flew solo across the Atlantic. Now a national celebrity, her success was celebrated with a parade through New York City and a reception at the White House. She was the first woman to be awarded the U.S. Distinguished Flying Cross.

Her most famous voyage was her last. Amelia set off from California in an attempt to become the first person to circumnavigate the Earth at the equator. Flying from the city of Lae in New Guinea to Howland Island, Amelia disappeared, never to be seen again. The mystery of her death has interested millions, but truly it was Amelia's determination to fly higher, travel farther, and prove that women are just as capable as men that keeps her memory and spirit alive today.

**1897**
Born in Atchison, Kansas, USA.

**1920**
Experienced her first flight.

**1921**
Bought her first plane.

"Women must try to do things as men have tried. When they fail, their failure must be but a challenge to others."

**1928**
Amelia was the first woman to cross the Atlantic in a plane.

**1931**
Married George Putnum, the publisher of her autobiography.

**1932**
Was the first women to fly solo over the Atlantic.

**1937**
Disappeared near Howland Island.

# Junko Tabei

Junko Tabei was a Japanese mountaineer. She was the first woman to climb to the top of Mount Everest, and the first to climb all Seven Summits— the highest peak on every continent.

Junko had her first taste of mountain climbing when she was ten years old, on a school trip to Mount Nasu. But she came from a big family with not very much money, so it was too expensive a hobby for her to keep up. She didn't climb much until she went to college and joined the mountain climbing club.

After college she set up the Ladies Climbing Club (LCC), the first of its kind in Japan. Junko felt the need for a women-only club because she was tired of the way male mountaineers treated her, not taking her seriously and assuming she was only there to find a husband. Some even refused to climb with her. All she wanted to do was enjoy climbing the mountains the same as anyone.

The LCC started a project to raise funds to climb Mount Everest. Junko helped to get sponsorship for the group from a newspaper and a television company—though she was often told that as a woman she should be raising children rather than climbing mountains.

The group then started training, and in 1975 began their expedition. When they were 20,600 feet up the mountain, an avalanche struck and buried the women and guides under snow. Junko was unconscious for six minutes but was rescued by her Sherpa guide. That did not frighten or stop her. Twelve days later, Junko became the first woman to reach the summit of Everest.

In later years, while still climbing, Junko worked to preserve the ecology of mountain environments. In college she studied the damage that can be done by trash left behind by climbers; she led "clean-up" climbs in Japan and the Himalayas, and was involved in a project to build an incinerator to burn mountain trash.

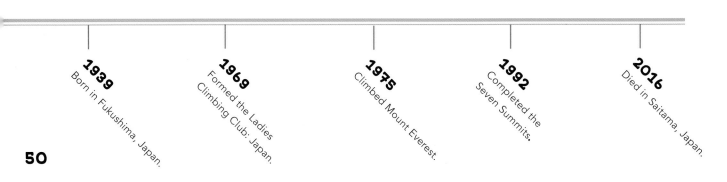

**1939**
Born in Fukushima, Japan.

**1969**
Formed the Ladies Climbing Club: Japan.

**1975**
Climbed Mount Everest.

**1992**
Completed the Seven Summits.

**2016**
Died in Saitama, Japan.

# Meryl Streep

Meryl Streep is one of the finest actors of her generation, known for her ability to perform all kinds of different roles and never sticking to one type.

Growing up, Meryl's mother was very supportive, and if Meryl lacked confidence would remind her: "If you're lazy, you're not going to get it done. But if you put your mind to it, you can do anything."

In high school, Meryl acted in plays but didn't take acting seriously until she was in college. After her degree, she studied for an MFA at Yale School of Drama, where she took on waitressing and typing jobs to earn money.

Her acting career quickly got off to a good start on the stage. It wasn't the same for her first movie experience though, which she hated because the film was edited so differently from how she had acted. She also wasn't always appreciated at auditions: the director of King Kong said in Italian that he thought she was

> "When the powerful use their position to bully, we all lose."

ugly—but Meryl understood Italian and rather than be embarrassed, responded that she couldn't do anything about how she looked.

She became known for playing roles of difficult or unlikable people. In 1979, she won a Golden Globe and an Oscar for Best Supporting Actress for her role in *Kramer vs Kramer*, where she played a mother who leaves her husband and young son. Meryl thought that her role was "too evil" so she persuaded the director to revise the script and let her write some of her own dialogue.

When Meryl was in her forties, she struggled to find interesting roles. But in *The Bridges of Madison County* she played an Italian farm wife, making her the first middle-aged actress to be taken seriously as a Hollywood romantic heroine.

As she got older she became celebrated for more varied films, with smash hits such as *The Devil Wears Prada* and *Mamma Mia!*

Her fame and wealth have enabled her to support two academic scholarships at the University of Massachusetts Lowell, and fund support for female scriptwriters over forty.

**1949**
Born in Summit, New Jersey, USA.

**1975**
Graduated with an MFA from Yale School of Drama.

**1980**
Won first Oscar, for Best Supporting Actress, in Kramer vs Kramer.

**1983**
Won Best Actress Oscar for Sophie's Choice.

**2012**
Won Best Actress Oscar for The Iron Lady.

**2017**
Awarded the Golden Globe Cecil B. DeMille Award.

# Bette Davis

**B**ette Davis was one of Hollywood's greatest actresses, playing a hundred plus roles over six decades. She was lauded for her portrayal of unlikable characters, such as Jane in *Whatever Happened to Baby Jane*. She often played the part of strong women, which reflected the strength of her own character.

Ruth Elizabeth Davis grew up in Lowell, Massachusetts. She was given the nickname "Betty," short for Elizabeth. She later changed the spelling of it to "Bette" after the French novel *La Cousine Bette* by Balzac. As a child, Bette was a Girl Scout and attended Cushing Academy where she was introduced to theater.

Bette started her movie career with Universal Studios, but the three films she made there weren't successful. She had almost given up on Hollywood when Warner Bros. put her in the lead role for *The Man Who Played God*, which became her big break. She stayed with Warner Bros. for the next eighteen years. By the late 1930s Bette was the studio's most profitable star.

While playing Queen Elizabeth I, Charles Laughton, who had played Henry VIII some years before, visited her on set one day. Bette confessed, "I have nerve trying to play Elizabeth I at my age!" (Bette was only thirty herself.) Laughton replied, "Never stop daring to hang yourself, Bette." This became her motto throughout her career: attempt the impossible in order to improve your work.

It was daring of Bette to take on so many unlikable characters. Most actresses of the time wanted to play kind or beautiful woman, but Bette knew that playing a range of characters would show the breadth of her acting ability.

It was one such role that first brought her critical acclaim. Mildred Rogers, Bette's character in *Of Human Bondage*, was vicious and hard. Bette chose to look realistic during Mildred's death scene, suffering from consumption, poverty, and neglect. *Life* magazine said Bette's was "probably the best performance ever recorded on the screen by a US actress," but she was overlooked for an Academy nomination. There was uproar from the press and fellow actors, and she won the Oscar for her next role, in *Dangerous*, but Bette considered it a consolation prize.

While Bette was a popular person on most sets, she could also be difficult to work with. On films she liked, she was well prepared and worked hard on finding her character. But her contract with Warner Bros. meant she sometimes had to work on films she hated—and then she behaved less well, even making up her lines while filming.

Bette was the first person to receive ten Oscar nominations. She won two Oscars, an Emmy, and over 100 awards during her career. She was very proud and honored to receive the Distinguished Civilian Service Medal, from the US Department of Defense, for creating the Hollywood Canteen. During World War II, the Los Angeles area was the embarkation point for thousands of service men who wanted to see Hollywood stars before being shipped out.

**1908**
Born in Lowell, Massachusetts, USA.

**1932**
The Man Who Played God was released.

**1934**
Of Human Bondage was released.

**1935**
Won Oscar for Best Actress for Dangerous.

"Attempt the impossible in order to improve your work."

1938
Won Oscar for Best Actress for Jezebel.

1941
Became first female President of the Academy of Motion Picture Arts and Sciences.

1977
Received the American Film Institute's Lifetime Achievement Award.

1980
Awarded Distinguished Civilian Service Medal.

1989
Died in Paris, France.

# Mary Pickford

Mary Pickford was a Canadian-American actress and film producer at the start of the movie industry. She was a founder of the Academy of Motion Picture Arts and Sciences, who organized the "Oscars."

Mary was born in Toronto in 1892 with the name Gladys Smith. After her father died, Gladys's mother took in lodgers to make money. One was a theater stage manager, who suggested that Gladys, aged seven, act in a one of his plays. This was the start of Gladys's acting career.

In the 1900s, Gladys and her family toured the United States performing, but they never made much money. Gladys dreamed of playing a leading Broadway role. In 1907 her dream came true, but the producer insisted that she change her name to Mary Pickford.

After Broadway, Mary auditioned for a part in a film. The director hired her—paying her a much better rate than most actors of the time. Mary worked very hard, knowing that the more films she appeared in the more famous she'd be. In 1909 she had appeared in fifty-one films.

In those days, actors weren't known by name. Her films advertised that they featured "the girl with the golden curls" or "Blondilocks." In 1914, her name was advertised for the first time. As the 1910s and 20s went on, she became possibly the most famous woman in the world. She negotiated a record-breaking salary of $10,000 a week.

In 1919 she cofounded a new production company, United Artists, with Charlie Chaplin and Douglas Fairbanks, two other major stars of the day. It revolutionized the US film industry, giving greater creative control to actors and producers. Mary was the most powerful woman ever to work in Hollywood.

When sound was added to films, Mary became less popular. She retired from acting in 1933 but continued to produce films. She used her fortune and influence to support good causes and set up the Mary Pickford Foundation in the 1950s.

**1892**
Born in Ontario, Canada.

**1907**
Acted the lead role in The Warrens of Virginia on Broadway.

**1919**
Cofounded United Artists.

**1921**
Founded the Motion Picture Relief Fund.

**1930**
Won the Oscar for her role in Coquette.

**1933**
Retired from acting.

**1979**
Died in California, USA.

# Emma Watson

Emma Watson is a British actress and activist, best known for her role as Hermione in the *Harry Potter* films. Before acting in *Harry Potter*, her only acting had been in school plays. Now, she is a globally famous actress and an influencer for young people in women's rights.

Emma was born in Paris to English parents, and lived there until she was five. When her parents split up, she moved to Oxfordshire with her mother. She did very well in school and enjoyed spending her free time at a stage school, learning singing, dancing, and acting.

It was her acting teacher who suggested Emma audition for the role of Hermione Granger in *Harry Potter*, and after eight auditions she was given the part. Recording the films took ten years and changed Emma's life forever in terms of fame, critical acclaim, and money.

By 2007 her roles in the *Harry Potter* series had earned Emma so much that she said she would never have to work for money again. She

> "If we stop defining ourselves by what we are not and start defining ourselves by what we are, we can be freer."

enrolled at Brown University in Rhode Island, USA, but she did act again—and her filming schedules meant it took her five years to earn her degree rather than four.

Soon after graduating, Emma became a UN Women Goodwill Ambassador and launched their global campaign for gender equality, called HeForShe. Her impassioned speech calling for equal rights and opportunities so inspired Malala Yousafzai that, she says, she decided to call herself a feminist after hearing Emma's speech.

As an extension of her UN work, in 2016 Emma started a feminist book group called *Our Shared Shelf*, with the aim of bringing feminist thought to people everywhere. Every two months she chooses a book on equality and everyone, regardless of gender, is encouraged to read along with her and then join a discussion in the online forum.

Her passion for engaging as many people as possible in issues of equality is personal and authentic and she uses her fame and wealth to find new and interesting ways of doing so.

**1990**
Born in Paris, France

**2001**
*Harry Potter and the Sorcerer's Stone* was released.

**2011**
*Harry Potter and the Deathly Hallows— Part 2* was released.

**2014**
Graduated from Brown University with a degree in English literature.

**2014**
Launched the UN's HeForShe campaign for gender equality.

**2016**
Launched Our Shared Shelf.

# Instructions

All of your characters have the same basic body, so the instructions are the same for each person. Press out the pieces carefully so that you don't tear anything. The pieces are pre-creased, so you can gently fold them into shape.

## HEAD

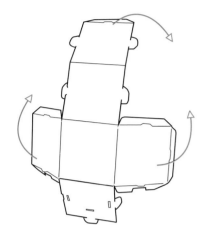

Face of the model is here

Leave open

- Take the head and gently fold all the creases so that it forms a box.
- Slot the tabs on the top of the head into the side. Fold up the bottom, but leave the back open.

## BODY

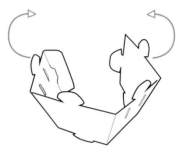

- Take the body and fold the creases so that it forms a box.
- Slot in the tab to hold the box together.

## ARMS

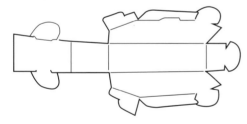

- Fold the creases as shown to form a tube.

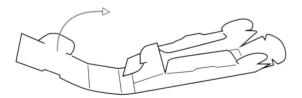

- Slot the tabs together.

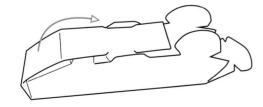

- Fold over the long end and slot the tabs in.
- Repeat for the second arm.

## LEGS

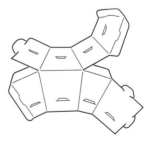

- Fold the creases to form a box as shown.
- Slot the tab to hold the lower and upper sections together.

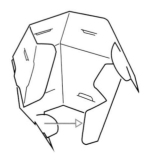

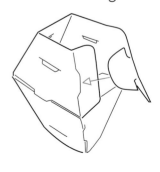

- Slot in the tab to hold the lower section together.
- Slot in the tab on the upper section.

# FEET

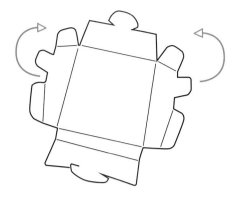

Fold up the sides and ends.

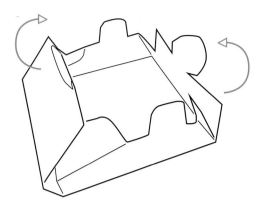

The feet should look like this ready to slot into the legs.

# PUTTING YOUR MODEL TOGETHER

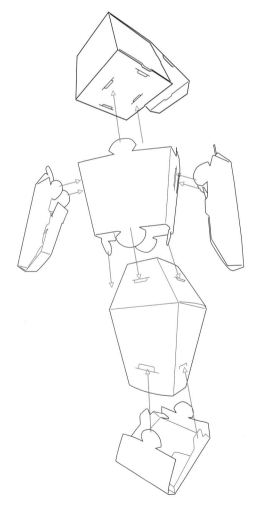

# FINISHED FIGURE

Leave the back of the head open.

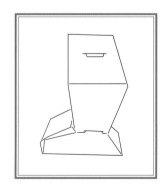

The feet and legs should look like this.

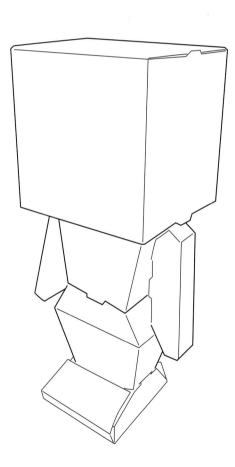

Now that you know how to build the body, turn the page to build each figure's unique features.

- Starting at the bottom, slot the feet onto the legs.
- Slot the legs and feet onto the bottom of the body.
- Slot the arms onto each side of the body.
- Carefully slot the tabs on the top of the arms and body into the head.
- Once together, fold down the back of the head and close.

# FRIDA KAHLO

Frida Kahlo took great care with her style as it was one way in which she asserted her identity. Her model includes one of her iconic headdresses.

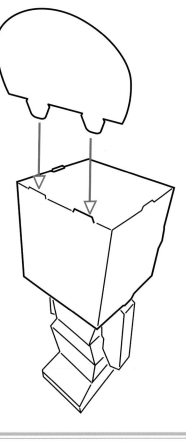

- Slot the tabs on the hair into the two slots on the top of the head.

**TIP**
Open up the back of the head to pull the tabs through more easily.

MODEL
SHEET
2

# QUEEN ELIZABETH I

Queen Elizabeth I is dressed for court in a sumptuous dress with a ruff, a crown, and jewels.

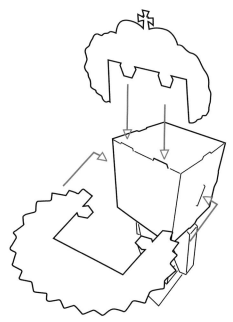

- Slot the tabs on the hair into the two slots on the top of the head.

- The ruff slots into the side of the head.

# MAYA ANGELOU

Maya Angelou frequently wore a headscarf, which was known as her signature look. She carries a copy of her first best-selling memoir.

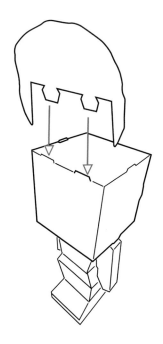

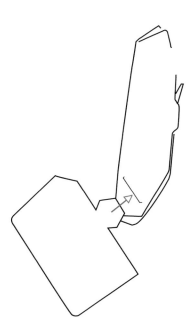

- Slot the tabs on the hair into the two slots on the top of the head.

- Slot the tab on the book into the slot on the side of the arm.

# ROSALIND FRANKLIN

Rosalind Franklin stands next to her microscope and holds "Photograph 51," the x-ray she took which led to the discovery of double helix DNA.

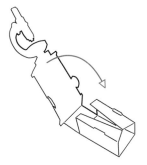

- Take the microscope and fold the creases into a box.

- Fold the long section over the box.

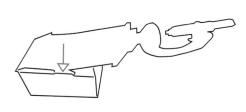

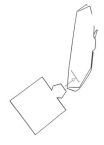

- Slide the tabs into the slots in the box section.

- Slide the tabs on the photo into the slot in the arm.

# ALTHEA GIBSON

Althea Gibson is ready to win another match in her tennis whites and holds her tennis racket.

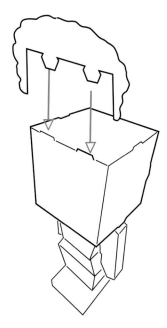

- Slot the tabs on the hair into the two slots on the top of the head.

- Slot the tab on the tennis racket into the slot on the side of the arm.

# ROSA PARKS

Rosa Parks is wearing her glasses and carrying a bus token, as she was when she embarked on that life-changing bus ride.

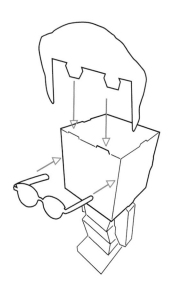

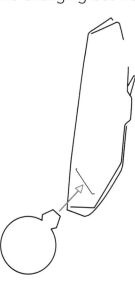

- Slot the tabs on the hair into the two slots on the top of the head.

- Fold the arms on the glasses and slot them into each side of the head.

- Slot the tab on the token into the slot on the side of the arm.

# FLORENCE NIGHTINGALE

Florence Nightingale is in her nurse's uniform and carries her lantern, ready to look after the soldiers in her care.

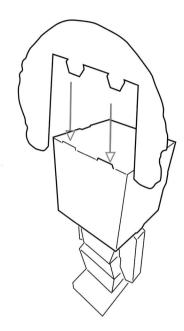
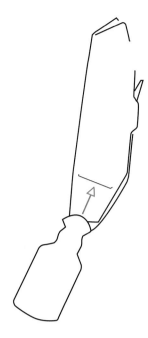

- Slot the tabs on the hair into the two slots on the top of the head.

- Slot the tab on the lamp into the slot on the side of the arm.

# ELLA FITZGERALD®

Ella Fitzgerald is dressed up for a show with her hair piled high and with her microphone is ready to sing the blues.

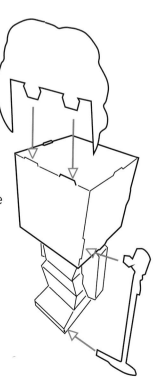

- Slot the tabs on the hair into the two slots on the top of the head.

- There are two slots on the microphone. Slot the top one into the side of the head and the bottom one into the side of the feet.

# AMELIA EARHART

Amelia Earhart is in her flight jacket, helmet and goggles, about to embark on a solo flight across the Atlantic Ocean.

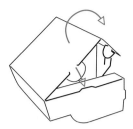

- Fold the sides of the helmet around and the top down. Slot the tabs in place.

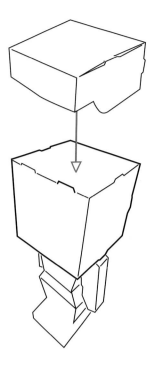

- Fold the back of the helmet down and slot the tabs in place.

- Place the helmet on top of the head.

# BETTE DAVIS

Bette Davis is dressed for her role as Arlene Bradford in the film *Fog Over Frisco*, in 1934.

- Slot the tabs on the hair into the two slots on the top of the head.

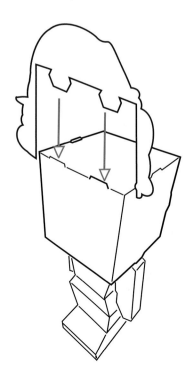

# Index

## Picture Credits

**Alamy** p8 Jerónimo Alba

**Getty** p12 Imagno / Contributor, p18 Michael Ochs Archives / Stringer, p22 Universal History Archive / Contributor, p28 Bettmann / Contributor, p32 Universal ImagesGroup / Contributor, p38 March Of Time / Contributor, p42 Michael Ochs Archives / Stringer, p48 Pictures Inc. / Contributor, p52 Silver Screen Collection / Contributor